Pearson Baccalaureate PYP Readers

Mzungu

Kelly Cunnane

Pearson Education Limited is a company incorporated in England
and Wales, having its registered office at Edinburgh Gate, Harlow,
Essex, CM20 2JE. Registered company number: 872828

www.pearsonglobalschools.com

Text © Kelly Cunnane 1994

This edition published by Pearson Education Ltd in 2009

20 19 18
IMP 13 12 11 10

British Library Cataloguing in Publication Data
A catalogue record for this book is available from the British
Library.

ISBN 978 0 435996 16 1

Printed in China (CTPSC/10)

Kugo, Kibet's grandfather, was praying to the morning sun. It was just rising over the gardens of the village. Then he wakened his grandson. Kibet was asleep beneath a cowskin on the bamboo bed.

'Kibet, wake up. I am going down to the valley today. You must watch my cows.'

'I'm very hungry,' Kibet said, and he went to Mama's round mud hut. Milk for tea was heating on the fire.

Mama stirred the porridge with a stick between her hands. Kibet ate his food quickly.

'Your sister is waiting for you,' Mama said.

Jelagat, his little sister, had a long stick to drive the cows to the hillside.

Kibet and Jelagat walked after the
lazy cows, zigzagging across the green,
green hills.

'Look over there,' Kibet shouted.

Across the little valley, a ball of dust
rolled along the road to the village.

'Let's go and see who is coming,'
Jelagat shouted.

They ran across to the road and saw
a truck stop at the school. The driver
climbed up on top of the truck. He
threw down a big sack and a box.

Then something climbed down from inside the truck. The children had never seen anything like it. They were too astonished to run away. They just stared.

'Is it a ghost?' screamed Jelagat, jumping behind her brother.

'Look at its skin! It's the colour of milk!' Kibet whispered.

'Look at the long fur on the top of its head,' said Jelagat, holding on to Kibet. 'It's like the monkey fur on Kugo's dance hat. Do you think it will eat us?'

'Hello,' said the white ghost. 'Do you know where the principal of the school lives?'

The ghost's eyes had no colour, like the stream at the bottom of the hill. The children hid behind the truck.

'Hello,' the ghost said again. The children ran as fast as they could to Mama's hut.

'Mama, Mama, we saw a *mzungu*, a white stranger. It chattered like a monkey,' Kibet shouted.

'Oh, that must be the new teacher,' said Mama, not frightened at all.

She poured them a mug of milk
from a gourd hung on the wall. It was
sweetened with charcoal, and it was
cool and tasty.

Suddenly Kibet remembered. Kugo's
cows! Where were they?

He ran outside. They weren't on the hill. They weren't beneath the blue gum trees.

Kibet ran past the village shop. Maybe the cows were in someone's garden. Kugo would be very angry. Kibet ran down the hill.

Maybe the cows were thirsty. He ran
as fast as he could to the river.

He heard the sound of someone
splashing, and saw the white stranger
– the *mzungu*.

Kibet quickly hid in the bushes.

'Get away! Shoo!' shouted the stranger.

Kibet looked through the leaves. One of the cows had its nose in the *mzungu*'s basket of clothes. It pulled out a shirt and began to chew it.

'Give me that!' the *mzungu* shouted, waving its arms. Its long hair flew around its head.

One cow began to eat the soap powder for washing the clothes. Another one stood on the clothes drying on the ground.

'Help!' shouted the *mzungu*.

Kibet began to laugh. He picked up a stick and chased the stupid cows up the hill.

The *mzungu* shouted something, but Kibet didn't hear. It sounded like '*asante*'. *Asante* is 'thank you' in the language of the village.

The cows were safe and Jelagat was very happy. Kibet told her about the *mzungu* and they rolled in the grass laughing.

'Come here,' their mother shouted. 'Go to the garden and bring a cabbage and some potatoes and carrots.'

She put the food in a big basket.
Then she gave Jelagat a jug of milk. It
was still warm from the cow.

'Take this to the new teacher's house
next to the school,' their mother said.
'Welcome her. Bring back the jug.'

Go to the *mzungu*'s house! Oh no!

They walked very slowly. They made drawings in the dust. They picked flowers to suck on.

'Look! A dung beetle!' They watched it. It rolled a ball of dung into its hole.

Jelagat began to cry.

'I don't want to go to the ghost's house,' she said.

Kibet put the basket down and caught some flying insects.

'These are sweet,' he said, and put some in his mouth. Jelagat stopped crying and caught some too.

'Let's leave everything at the door and run,' Kibet said. They were standing in front of the *mzungu*'s house.

'No! We have to bring the jug back,' whispered Jelagat.

'*Jambo*,' a voice said. *Jambo* means 'hello'.

The door opened. It was the ghost.

'Is this for me?' it said in its monkey chatter. 'I'm very hungry, and I've nothing to eat in the house.'

The *mzungu* took the things and put them on the table.

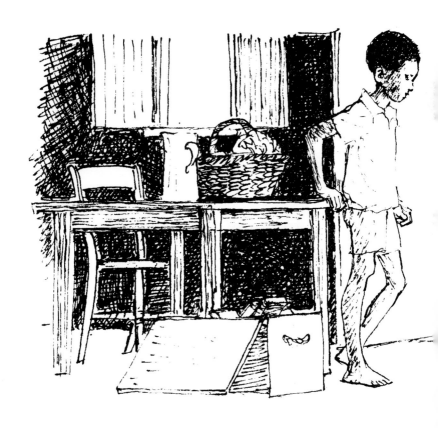

'A table!' Kibet whispered. 'We don't
have a table in our hut.'

'I don't see a cooking fire,' Jelagat
whispered back.

The children looked around. There
was a box on the floor. It was full of
books. Jelagat loved books.

Suddenly the *mzungu* knelt in front
of them.

'*Asante*,' she said. 'Thank you.'

Then she asked them their names in
their own language. They were too shy
to answer.

'You can call me Teacher,' she said.

They looked at the teacher. Her eyes were blue and her skin was pink not white. Her hair was long and silky. She had a nice smile. But her voice still made the children laugh. It was high and chattering, like a monkey's voice.

Now Jelagat was able to speak. 'Please, Mama wants the jug.'

The teacher got up and emptied the milk into a white bowl. Then she washed the jug with water from a large bucket.

'She understands you,' Kibet whispered in surprise.

'Thank you, my little friends,' the
teacher said. She gave Jelagat the jug.

'Thank you,' Jelagat said. 'We will
come back in the morning. You will
need help. We will show you the shop.'

They ran out of the house and along
the road.

Jelagat stopped. She looked back at the little house. Kibet stopped and looked too. The teacher was standing alone at the door. She waved to them.

'*Karibu*! Welcome!' Jelagat shouted.

'Welcome!' Kibet shouted.

The teacher smiled and waved again.

Questions

1 What is Kibet doing when his grandfather calls him?
2 What does Kugo want Kibet to do?
3 Why do Kibet and Jelagat leave the cows and go into the village?
4 What do they see?
5 Why are they astonished?
6 What are the cows doing when Kibet finds them?
7 Why does Mama give Kibet and Jelagat a basket of food and a jug of milk?
8 Why do they draw in the dust, pick flowers and watch the dung beetle?
9 How does the story end?

Activities

1 Draw a picture of Kibet and Jelagat just as they look when they first see the *mzungu*.
2 Write a short story about two children who meet a strange creature they have never seen before.
3 The Yeti in the Himalayas and Big Foot in the western USA are strange creatures which people say exist. Find out what they are and then find out if there are any other strange creatures which people have talked about.

Glossary

astonished (page 6) very surprised

bamboo (page 1) thick canes – they look like sugar cane

chattered (page 9) made quick noises like a monkey, spoke very quickly

dung beetle (page 18) a large black beetle which lays its eggs in dung

mzungu (cover page) a Kiswahili word for a white person

silky (page 24) very soft and smooth, like silk

zigzagging (page 4) not going in straight lines, going first one way and then the other